BUD NEILL's

LOBEY DOSSER

FURTHER ADVENTURES OF THE WEE BOY!

FOREWORD BY TOM SHIELDS   **INTRODUCED BY RANALD MACCOLL**

ZIPO
PUBLISHING

First published in Great Britain in 1998 by
ZIPO PUBLISHING LIMITED
4 Cowan Street, Glasgow, G12 8PF

website: www.zipo.co.uk
e-mail: info@zipo.co.uk

ISBN 1 901984 00 1

Other ZIPO titles available:
Bud Neill's Magic! ISBN 1 901984 01 X

A catalogue for this book is available from the British Library

Original cover design by Ranald MacColl
Five story introduction pages drawn by Malky McCormick
Lobey Dosser statue photograph by Eleanor Barron
"Lobey Dosser - Space Traveller" cuttings supplied by Warren Brown
Additional source material from The Mitchell Library, Glasgow

Printed and bound in Great Britain by The Cromwell Press, Wiltshire

CONTENTS

FOREWORD 5

INTRODUCTION 11

CAST O' THOOSANS 15

THE MAGIC HORSESHOE 21

THE HAUNTED FORT 63

THE CALTON CREEK CAUR 81

LOBEY DOSSER - SPACE TRAVELLER 113

THE LAST RIDE 145

FOREWORD

The statue of Lobey Dosser in Woodlands Road, Glasgow, can lay claim to two firsts. It is the world's only two-legged equestrian statue*. It is also the only statue in Britain since Victorian times to be erected by public subscription**.

The above claims may or may not be accurate but what is true is that it is Glasgow's best-loved statue. The wee horse's nose is shiny from the many friendly pats it has received since it was unveiled in 1992. Lobey astride his faithful steed El Fideldo brings a smile to the faces of all who pass by and is thus a fitting tribute to newspaper cartoonist Bud Neill.

Neill entertained readers for three decades with his surreal Lobey Dosser strips and pithy pocket cartoons. He died in 1970 and his humour became a fond memory. In the mid-1970s, so forgotten a figure had Bud Neill become that when the Daily Express newspaper closed their Glasgow print centre, dozens of bin bags of his original work were thrown out as rubbish.

Fortunately, Calum MacKenzie happened to be in the Express Bar pub adjacent to a skip containing some of the Neill works and these were saved for posterity. At around the same time, Ranald MacColl, another Glasgow artist, had begun the task of saving Bud Neill memorabilia and of interviewing friends and colleagues of the great man with a view, one day, to publishing a biography.

We flash forward to the year 1989 when the city of Glasgow was preparing to be European City of Culture 1990. It was to be a year when Glasgow was loupin' with art of every shape and form. A few dissenting voices asked: "What about Glasgow's own culture?". Over a pint or more in the Halt Bar, Calum MacKenzie and friends came up with the idea of a statue of Bud Neill's most famous character. In his own inimitable style, Calum sub-contracted the actual job to the Glasgow Herald Diary column.

An appeal was launched in the columns of the Diary which produced not only the £10,000 projected budget for the statue but also a flood of readers' memories of magic moments from the pen of Bud Neill. It was the start of a revival of interest in Neill's work which was consolidated by exhibitions of his work. Dr Sam McKinlay, editor of the Evening Times who was the first to spot Bud Neill's talent wrote: "I am glad the appeal has gone so well although I have a sneaking feeling that Bud should have been commemorated otherwise. I imagine it's going to be awfully difficult explaining the reason for the statue when it does appear." Cliff Hanley, the journalist, wit, wee smart Alec, and contemporary of Neill, also doubted whether Bud would have appreciated having a statue in his memory.

It seemed that other forces were also conspiring against the project. The £10,000 budget, compiled on the back of an envelope in the Halt Bar, was about £10,000 short of the actual cost. Some wheeling and dealing was done to raise a further £8,000 but what made the Lobey Dosser statue a reality was the arrival on the scene of Tony Morrow and Nick Gillon, two students at Duncan of Jordanstone College of Art in Dundee. They designed and built the statue for no fee but as a challenge to their passion and commitment to figurative sculpture. They had never even seen a Bud Neill cartoon far less a Lobey Dosser strip but they were lucky to have Bill Ritchie, a Dundee cartoonist and great fan of Bud Neill, as adviser.

Whether or not Neill would approve of the statue, we do not know. But we think he might be entertained by the reaction to it. We think he might like the fact that this cheeky stookie is the first thing the faithful from the nearby Free Kirk see when they come out of their services. Many weans have been photographed sitting on Lobey's knee. Students use it as a backdrop for their graduation pictures. The statue's corner location makes it ideal for a wee seat on the plinth as a fish supper, or some other morsel, is consumed. The new laws prohibiting the al fresco consumption of alcohol in Glasgow have prevented its continued use as a gathering place for the thirsty.

The Lobey statue is now firmly on the tourist track. It is always entertaining to watch passing Italians, Japanese, and many other puzzled nationalities trying to work out what on earth it is all about. Only Bud Neill could have come up with a cartoon strip in which Glasgow and its humour is transported to the Arizona desert. Only Glasgow could build a statue to thank him for doing so.

At the height of the fund-raising campaign, the Herald Diary was receiving 500 letters a week on the subject of Bud Neill and all his works. We still get the odd communication, like the one from the Glasgow man, long an exile in London. He wrote to express his thanks that the statue had been built and that its unveiling had been reported in The Guardian with a full background about Bud Neill, Lobey Dosser and company. For many a year, usually at Hogmanay time, our London exile would become maudlin and would talk about the Glasgow of his youth in general and Lobey Dosser in particular. His children, brought up in England would merely say:"There's Dad on the whisky again." "Now, they know I wasn't raving," he wrote.

The statue is not only decorative but is also useful. We hear of an Irishman who was in Glasgow recently visiting friends. After a night out in various pubs, he was trying to make his way back to his chum's flat in the West End. He realised he had gone too far west when he saw countryside and signs for Balloch. He stopped a taxi but did not know which street he was looking for. He had only one bit of knowledge of Glasgow which could get him home. "This may sound as if I'm really drunk," he said to the taxi driver, " but I'm looking for my pal's flat. It overlooks a statue of a two-legged horse." "Lobey Dosser. Woodlands Road," the driver said and the Irishman was duly delivered.

Tom Shields, 1998

* Source: Calum MacKenzie, the Glasgow artist who
came up with the original concept of the statue.

**Source: The Guardian Newspaper.

The bronze statue of Lobey Dosser, Rank Bajin and El Fideldo which is situated on Woodlands Road, Glasgow.

The inscription on the plinth reads:

Statue erected by public subscription on May 1st 1992 to the memory of

BUD NEILL

1911-1970

CARTOONIST & POET

Creator of Lobey Dosser, Sheriff of Calton Creek, his trusty steed El Fideldo, resident villain Rank Bajin, and many other characters.

INTRODUCTION

The time is high noon, 1949. The location is Calton Creek. A Shangri-la 1880's style hamlet nestled beneath the slopes of an Arizona sandstone butte. The only brisk movement on the clinker built faceted main street is a scurrying tumbleweed caught by a dust devil. The boardwalks percuss to the sound of Cuban heels and spurs. The clip-clop iron shoes of a passing horse stir a cloud of red dust which settles on the shoulders and Stetson of a snoozing cowboy.

A clutch of wee women are chewing the fat at a street corner seemingly anchored to the spot by their bulky shopping bags; a screaming toddler is tucked under an arm. Round their coat waists are *gunbelts?* Overheard is the unmistakable stuccato tones of *Glaswegian accents?*

Further down the main street a shingle announces: "Rank Bajin. Resident Villain. Bad deeds done. Distance no object." Across the dusty street is the Sheriff's office. Tied to and leaning against the hitching post is a *biped* horse? It's legs are crossed. The sound of a picked guitar resonates from the open door. It is the Sheriff: one Lobey Dosser. A person of pre-national health stature, that is wee. He has a bad eye, a button nose and a beard Santa Claus would give his eye teeth for. No one would blame the onlooker for thinking he had had one pyote too many.

This is no ordinary Western. But then, Bud Neill, the creator of Lobey Dosser was no ordinary artist.

He had already established a large following due to his quirky pocket cartoons which appeared in the Evening Times during the previous five years. His freshly original and sometimes surreal view of Glaswegian's mores and foibles caught the citizens' imaginations and when the newspaper announced that Bud had created a Western strip the readership eagerly anticipated its launch. It's success was a foregone conclusion with fans ranging from Lawyers and students to shipyard workers.

The stories in this volume cover the decade in which Lobey rode across the newsprint. They show the changes in styles with which Bud experimented. He was in the true sense an artist, with an enquiring and creative mind which could not content itself with churning out a conventional form day after day, no matter how successful it might be.

Although the Lobey Dosser stories were of the Western genre, he saw no contradiction in introducing storylines and plots which were of no relevance to the cowboy theme. He was a keen cineaste and some of the subject matter in these stories reflect that influence. The 1951 story, "The Haunted Fort" features a Frankensteinesque monster who stalks two gallus girls named Roona and Noka Boot.

Although the 1950's film-goers' popular diet consisted of the Western, a new genre, the outer space adventure was fast becoming a rival due to the public's fascination of the advent of the new world nuclear age, rocketry and science. Bud's 1955 "Lobey Dosser - Space Traveller" involves Lobey et al in an extra-terrestrial journey to the far flung stars. But this is no "Star Wars" high-tech, special effects romp. It is given the Neillian treatment - the planets are made of corned beef and boiled cabbage.

The semi-realistic style of "The Calton Creek Caur" (1952), was a sign of Bud's early uneasiness at being typecast by the Lobey Dosser character. The public had made icons of the wee Sheriff and the other main protagonists of the newspaper cartoon. They had become more famous than their creator. Bud was beginning to feel trapped by the strip's popularity and this drawing style was by way of a rebellion against this. It was less well received than the usual format. In 1956 Bud moved from the Evening Times to the Daily Record and the Sunday Mail. He drew daily pocket cartoons for the record and, finally, was given a regular column to write - a dream of his for many years. He had, with some relief, left Lobey Dosser behind him at the Evening Times.

But in 1958 the Record management asked him to re-invent the wee Calton Creek Sheriff for the Sunday Mail. Two years had gone by and Bud no longer perceived Lobey as a creative burden. He agreed to a weekly strip.

Although the crisp and elegant pen and ink renditions illustrated Bud's undoubted mastery of the medium a serialised strip needs to maintain a momentum and the seven day gap proved to be fatal in this respect. The strip lasted less than a year.

Although Lobey exited with more of a phut than a bang, he has assured himself and, of course, his creator Bud Neill of a place in popular Glaswegian folklore.

Ranald MacColl, 1998

• • • • • •

I would like to thank the many people who were involved in the making of "Lobey Dosser - Further Adventures of the Wee Boy!", in particular: Yvonne Barron, Tony Hamill, Dave Alexander, Robert Thomson, Malky McCormick, Alex Ronald, Tom Shields, The Mitchell Library, Warren Brown, Colin MacMillan, Eleanor Barron, Christine Barron and, finally, the Neill family for their enduring support.

LOBEY DOSSER

Lobey Dosser is the Sheriff of Calton Creek. The scourge of the town's resident villain, Lobey's size and appearance belie a tenacity that has seen him through many a scrape. Lobey is over 21, unmarried and enjoys playing the moothie.

In short, "Lobey is the Wee Boy!".

EL FIDELDO

El Fideldo (or Elfie for short) is Lobey's two-legged trusty steed and best friend.

Unswerving in her loyalty to Lobey, Elfie won't let anyone other than Lobey on her back as even the toughest of bronco busters have found to their cost.

RANK BAJIN

Rank Bajin is the resident villain of Calton Creek.
With his proficient command of English, Rank Bajin's
"patter" is at odds with that of the Calton Creekers.
Charming and disarming, his prose is merely a guise
concealing a heart as black as his attire.

His age is unknown, he is married to Ima and has
four boys. He has a fondness for toasted cheese.

BIG CHIEF TOFFY TEETH

Toffy Teeth is the Chief of the Laya Bout tribe whose
lack of scruples would make even Rank Bajin blush.
He has formed an uneasy alliance with the
aforementioned villain to further their nefarious
deeds. Double dealing is most definitely the order of
the day with this Indian for whom no crime is too
heinous.

FAIRY NUFF

A pantomime fairy from Yoker, complete with magic wand and tackitty boots, Fairy Nuff astounds all with her magical prowess. Proud wife of Rid Skwerr and mother of four, she speaks only in rhyming verse.

RID SKWERR

A dutiful husband and loving father, this former foreign spy is now in the employ of Calton Creek Council haunting the town's cemetery. A happy soul, he considers himself to be "the luckiest spook in Arizona".

STARK STAIRN

A mysterious hermit, Stark Stairn comes to the aid of the Calton Creekers using his nuclear powered hat to power the town's tram "caur".

THE GI BRIDE

A forlorn figure, the GI Bride pops up in the most unlikely places with wee Ned and a large duffle bag in tow. Her efforts to hitchhike home are usually fruitless but on the odd occasion our intrepid Sheriff Dosser will speed her home to "Pertick".

DOKTOR ZOO

This German boffin leads our Sheriff on his most exciting adventure yet - travelling into deep space to the planet Zuz.

ROONA AND NOKA BOOT

A motley pair, Roona and Noka are soon in the thick of the action. These two sisters are not to be trifled with.

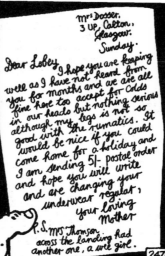

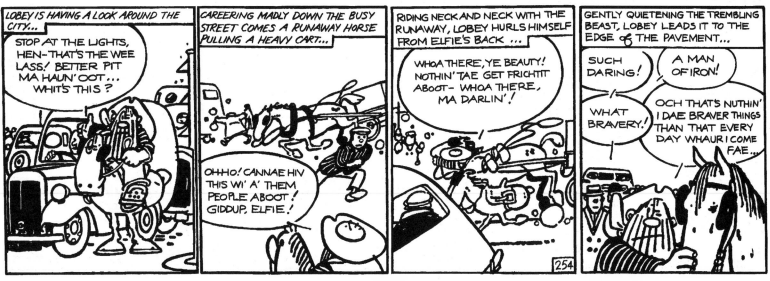

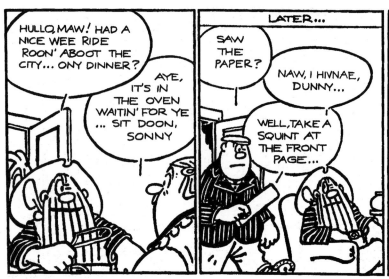

I'M RIGHT WORRIT ABOOT MY MAGIC HORSE-SHOE NO' WORKIN'... I'LL HIV TAE GET MONEY TAE GET BACK TO THE CREEK SOMEHOW— BUT WHERE, THAT'S THE BIT?

SOME TIME LATER...

HEAVENS, ELFIE– I'VE BEEN WORRYIN' THAT MUCH I HIVNAE LOOKED WHAUR WE WERE GOIN'! THIS IS US IN PERTICK— THE DUMBARTON ROAD

?

CAR STOP

HER SISTER, MAIR THAN LIKELY!

I'VE DECIDED TO STERT A CIRCUS IN THE BACK COORT, MAW... I'VE NAE MONEY TAE GET BACK TAE THE CREEK NOO THE MAGIC HORSE SHOE'S KNACKERED

OH AYE

A' I WID NEED IS A COUPLE O' CLOWNS... DUNNY COULD BE THE RINGMAISTER...

THAT'S RIGHT AYE

CHERGE A TANNER ADMISSION WI' A FREE MATINEE FOR THE WEANS ... AGGIE COULD PRINT THE POSTERS

SO SHE COULD UH-HUH

BUT WHAUR'LL I GET A COUPLE O' CLOWNS?

THERE'S PLENTY UP AT GEORGE SQUARE, YIR FAITHER SAYS...

ONE AFTERNOON WE FIND RANK BAJIN IN THE OLD CORRAL WITH HIS BIG BLACK STALLION 'TERROR'...

HERE, TERROR NICE TERROR PUTT, PUTT PUTT...

A FIERY, UNTAMED FURY IS 'TERROR', OVER WHOSE BACK NO MAN HAS EVER THROWN A BRIDLE - PROBABLY BECAUSE THAT AIN'T WHERE THEY THROW BRIDLES...

GOOD 'TERROR', NICE 'TERROR' ...CLUCK, CLUCK, CLUCK

NOBLE DESCENDANT OF THE PROUD BREED WHICH ROAMED THE RICH PASTURES OF THE OLD WEST CENTURIES BEFORE THE ADVENT OF THE RED MAN, THE BLACK STALLIONS FLATTENED EARS BETRAY HIS RESENTMENT AT BEING CONFINED IN BAJIN'S CORRAL WHEN HE COULD BE WORKING FOR METRO-GOLDWYN-SO...

WHAM

285

ONE AFTERNOON WE FIND RANK BAJIN LEAVING THE OLD CORRAL AND HIS BLACK STALLION, 'TERROR'...

THEM BOYS DOWN IN MEXICO IS SHORE EXPERIMENTIN' WIT SOME FANCY LOOKIN' ROCKETS THESE DAYS EB...

YUP

MADDENED BY THE CONFINING BARS OF THE CORRAL AND BY THE DUFF OATS WHICH HE HAS BEEN EATING 'TERROR' GALLOPS TOWARDS THE TEN FOOT BARRIER WHICH STANDS BETWEEN HIM AND FREEDOM...

THEN WITH EFFORTLESS EASE, SAILS OVER THE TOPMOST BAR AND HIGHTAILS IT FOR THE HILLS...

A QUARTER OF A MILE AWAY, BAJIN COMES INTO LAND...

286

THAT KICK BY 'TERROR' WAS A CRUEL BLOW TO MY PRESTIGE NOT TO MENTION ANOTHER PART OF MY ANATOMY - BUT WHAT A WONDERFUL HORSE! I MUST BREAK HIM AND TRAIN HIM FOR THE RODEO... THERE IS NO OTHER ANIMAL IN THE STATES TO TOUCH HIM, EXCEPT PERHAPS LASSIE...

BAJIN RETURNS TO HIS CORRAL ONLY TO FIND THAT THE BLACK STALLION, TERROR, HAS ESCAPED...

OH, TAP ME ON THE SCONCE WITH A HALF BRICK FOR NOT HAVING BUILT THE FENCE HIGHER—AND DASH AND TUSH, ALSO...

WITH THE DEPARTURE OF MY SPLENDID HORSE THE PROSPECT OF MY WINNING THE RODEO CHAMPIONSHIP IS CONSIDERABLY NIL, TO SAY THE LEAST OF IT—SO I WILL NOW PROCEED INTO TOWN AND DROWN MY SORROWS IN A NOGGIN OF PORT TYPE TUTTI-FRUTTI...

LATER....

WELL, TEAR OFF MY HOOD AND CALL ME HARRY LIME IF IT IS NOT MY FINE STALLION LOAFING AROUND DOSSER'S OFFICE!

BUD NEILL 289

THE NOBLE ANIMAL MUST HAVE A SLATE LOOSE TO EVEN BE SEEN OUTSIDE SUCH AN ESTABLISHMENT ... I WILL HAVE A WORD WITH THE SHERIFF ABOUT THIS...

I SEE MY NEW BLACK STALLION, 'TERROR' OUTSIDE YOUR DOOR DOSSER, AND PROPOSE TO REMOVE IT FROM THENCE WITH ALACRITY AND ALSO INSTANTER...

HE'S YOURS IS HE BAJIN? A FINE BIG BASTE...TAKE HIM AWA' HAME THEN

SLAM!

WHAM!

YE BACK ALREADY?

BUD 290

IT'S A SHAME TAE DAE IT TAE SUCH A NICE YOUNG BLOKE FOR HE'LL HIV TAE BE GUID TAE SIT ON 'TERROR'S' BACK ...BUT HE SAYS HE'S A CHAMPION BRONKY BUSTER, SO WE'LL SOON SEE...

THERE HE GOES NOO WI' HIS SADDLE ...'TERROR' WILL NO' LET HIM GET NEAR

EVERYBODY'S SCATTERED OOT THE ROAD ... BUT 'ACE' TAYLOR'S NO' FEART, THAT'S WAN THING — HE'S STILL GOIN' EFTER 'TERROR'

295

OH MERCIFUL GUIDNESS! 'ACE' TAYLOR'S FLUNG AWA' HIS SADDLE ...SURELY HE'S NO'

GOIN' TAE HIV A BASH ON 'TERROR' BARE-BACK!

YOUR WORST FEARS WILL BE CONFIRMED TO-MORROW, SHERIFF ...

BRONC BUSTER 'ACE' TAYLOR HAS NERVES OF STEEL — AND BEST SHEFFIELD STAINLESS AT THAT— FOR NEXT THING WE SEE IS 'ACE' ABOARD 'TERROR' THE FOUR-LEGGED TORNADO...

THE BIG BLACK STALLION HAS EVERY TRICK IN THE BOOK ... WILL 'ACE' STAY LONG ON THIS HEAVING HURRICANE OF HORSE FLESH? IT'S ANYBODY'S GUESS...

296

I DON'T KNOW ABOUT YOU, BUT I'M PUTTING MY MONEY ON 'ACE'

THERE! I HAVE FIRMLY STUCK ON THE TWO BACK LEGS...NOBODY WILL RECOGNISE IT AS DOSSERS HORSE, ESPECIALLY WITH THIS FALSE BEARD...

GLUE

EFTER...

FOUND YOUR PONY, YET, SHERIFF?

NAW, NAE SIGNS O' ELFIE...THIS A NEW YIN YE'VE GOT, BAJIN?

YES, I AM RIDING THIS HORSE IN THE RODEO ON MONDAY ...A CHARMING ANIMAL... GOOD DAY!

CHEERIO!

305

DOSSER DIDN'T RECOGNIZE HIS OWN HORSE! THE $10,000 IS PRACTICALLY IN THE BAG! ROLL ON MONDAY...

THE FIRST DAY OF THE RODEO...

BAJIN'S WON EVERY HEAT TODAY- THAT NEW PONY OF HIS IS A WONDER...

NEXT EVENT IS THE CALF-ROPIN'... HERE BAJIN COMIN' OOT NOO...

PROGRAMME

306

WAN O' THE LEGS HAS FELL OFF BAJIN'S HORSE.

OH, HEAVENS! THERE BOTH O' THEM AFF NOO! ONLY TWA LEGS... SAME AS ELFIE...

AWFUL TRUTH DAWNING A.T. ELFIE! IT IS ELFIE!

LOBEY SHOOTS ACROSS THE ARENA IN PURSUIT OF THE KNAVE BAJIN...

STOP THIEF! AN' GIE US BACK WUR HORSE

307

SUDDENLY AWARE OF WHAT HAS HAPPENED, BAJIN SETS ELFIE AT THE BARRIER...

STOP! THERE ELFIE'S FALSE BEARD'S BLEW AFF NEXT!

WE SAW WHAT HAPPENED, LOBEY WE'LL GO AFTER BAJIN... THE RODEO HAS BEEN DECLARED NULL AND ALSO VOID...

IT'S NAE USE — YE'LL NEVER CATCH UP WI' ELFIE

THE VERY THING! A WEE MOTOR BIKE! YOU BLOKES WAIT HERE AN' I'LL HIV BAJIN BACK IN A JIFFY...

HOT ON THE TRAIL OF BAJIN GOES LOBEY, UP HILL AND DOWN DALE ...

POP POP POP

308

TIRING OF THIS AFTER A FEW MILES HE GOES UP DALE AND DOWN HILL JUST FOR A WEE CHANGE...

POP POP POP POP POP

BY AN ASTONISHING COINCIDENCE, THE CALTON CREEK GENERAL ELECTION TAKES PLACE ON THURSDAY FEB 23RD ... ON THAT DAY THE CREEKERS WILL CAST THEIR VOTES IN FAVOUR OF ONE OR OTHER OF THE CONTESTING CANDIDATES — TWO EMINENT LOCAL GENTLEMEN IN DIFFERENT LINES OF BUSINESS, THEY ARE —

SHERIFF LOBEY DOSSER (Independent Criminal Abolitionist) CONFIDENTLY FIGHTING UNDER THE BANNER OF "FULL EMPLOYMENT FOR WUR FREE TEETH" THE SHERIFF IS HIGHLY REGARDED LOCALLY AS A HUMANITARIAN AND MILITANT CHAMPION OF THE OPPRESSED. HE IS 'OVER 21', UNMARRIED, AND SLEEPS WITH HIS HAT ON ...

'KEEP' THE HEID

RANKIN VON SCHTINKER BAJIN, Esq (Moderate, Terrorist): HAS A BIG FOLLOWING AMONG THE LOCAL REDSKINS TO WHOM HE SELLS SUBSIDISED FIRE-WATER AND CUT PRICE LEA-ENFIELDS. "END CONSCRIPTION AND DOSSER ALSO" IS HIS SLOGAN. AGE UNKNOWN, MARRIED, FOUR BOYS...

BANK ON RANK

311

A BITTER FIGHT IS PREDICTED, AND THE CALTON CREEK EMPORIUM IS DOING A ROARING TRADE IN OVER-RIPE FRUIT. BOTH CONTESTANTS WILL HOLD NUMEROUS PUBLIC MEETINGS FROM MONDAY UNTIL POLLING DAY A FULL REPORT OF WHICH WILL APPEAR WITH SICKENING REGULARITY IN THESE FRAMES...

FOR PURE HAVOC YE CANNAE WHACK A ROTTEN TURNIP...

LOBEY'S HIVIN' A MEETIN' AT THE CROSS THE NIGHT ... YE COMIN'?

WAIT TILL I PIT MA HAT ON...

AT THE CROSS...

ONY QUESTIONS AFORE I STERT MA SPEECH?

ASK YIR MAN, SIR — THEN VOTE FOR DOSSER

WHIT ABOOT WUR POST-WAR CREDITS?

WULL YE TAK A PENNY AFF THE LOAF?

AN HOUR LATER...

THE EES O' THE WORLD'S ON CALTON CREEK... BLAH, BLAH, ... CHAINS & FETTERS ... BLAH, BLAH, BLAH ...COULDNAE RUN A MENAGE... BLAH...

WHIT ABOOT WUR POST-WAR CREDITS?

312

IN BAJIN'S COMMITEE ROOMS...

MY SCOUTS REPORT THAT DOSSER'S MEETING'S ATTRACTING GREAT CROWDS. YOU BOYS GET DOWN THERE. YOU KNOW YOUR ORDERS...

YES, PAPA

BUD NEILL

ARE YE MEN OR MICE? ARE YE A BUNCH o' AULD WIVES? BLAH, BLAH, BLAH...

DISPERSE AMONG THE CROWD, BOYS! GOOD LUCK!

SOME MINUTES LATER...

FLING THE HALE BUNCH OOT... FLING THE HALE BUNCH ——

SLOSH!

HE GOT THE HALE BUNCH FLUNG, ALL RIGHT...

O' ROTTEN BANANIES, AYE...

A VERITABLE FUSILLADE...

EH?

WHIT ABOOT WUR POST-WAR CREDITS?

313

WHA DONE THAT?

THE FAIRIES!

WULL YE TAK' A PENNY AFF TOMATIES?

AT BAJIN'S COMMITTEE ROOMS...

WE ARE PLEASED TO REPORT, PAPA, THAT MR. DOSSER'S MEETING BROKE UP IN DISORDER AFTER OUR HAIL OF OVER-RIPE FRUIT STRUCK HIM WITH DEVASTATING EFFECT...

EXCELLENT MY BOYS! PAPA IS PROUD OF YOU!

WE HAVE WON A MORAL VICTORY! TOMORROW I WILL HOLD MY MEETING WHEN MY GIFTS AS AN ORATOR WILL SWAY THE ELECTORS... THEY WILL HANG ON MY EVERY WORD

INDEED THEY WILL, PAPA!

SO HAVE IT BRUITED ABOUT THIS HAMLET THAT THIS MODERATE TERRORIST CANDIDATE, MR. BAJIN, WILL ADDRESS THE CITIZENS AT THE CROSS TOMORROW NOON, SHARP

CERTAINLY PAPA!

314

AT LOBEY'S OFFICE...

IT'LL TAKE ME A WEEK TAE GET THAE TOMATTY SEEDS OOT MA BEARD... A FEEL RIGHT ROTTEN ABOUT THE HALE BUSINESS... TUT... TUT TUT WHIT A MESS...

BAJIN'S MEETING...

SO I ASK YOU TO PONDER CAREFULLY YOUR DIJUDICATION IN THIS MATTER AND TO TREAT WITH THE CONTEMPT IT DESERVES THE IMPUISSANT DIATRIBE OF THE OTHER CANDIDATE DOSSER...

AWFY DIDACTIC

EH?

WHIT ABOOT WUR POST WAR CREDITS?

NOW HAVING HEARKENED SO ATTENTIVELY TO MY ENUCLEATION OF THE PROBLEMS WHICH CONFRONT US ... BLAH, BLAH, BLAH ...

WHIT ABOOT WUR POST-WAR CREDITS?

SILENCE, WOMAN! KINDLY BUTTON YOUR FAT LIP YOU OBESE MOUNTAIN OF IGNORANCE!

BEVAN THE SECOND...

SO HE IS, AYE

315

I'LL MOUNTAIN O' IGGERANCE YE, YE, _WHACK_ - DIRTY... _BASH_, LOOKIN'... _CRACK_... ARTICLE... _WHAM_ ...THAT... _BANG_ ...YE ARE!

GUID AULD MAGGIE! GET TORE IN TAE HIM!

KICK HIS TEETH OOT!

IN BAJIN'S OFFICE

A FOUL ASSAULT ON A HELPLESS POLITICIAN...

INDEED IT WAS, PAPA...

IN LOBEY'S OFFICE...

THAT'S BETTER NOO - I'M ALL CLEANED UP ...COME IN!

KNOCK KNOCK

THERE'S ANITHER BLOKE STANDING LOBEY — A STRANGER ...

IS THAT A FAC'!

316

MEET THE OTHER CANDIDATE, FITZ O'COUGHIN ESQ (INDEPENDENT VOTE SPLITTER, A GENERAL GUMMER UPPER)

THIS FITZ O'COUGHLIN CHARACTER IS JUST OUT TO SPLIT THE VOTE — A LOW TRICK...

INDEED IT IS PAPA!

NOW LISTEN BOYS — I HAVE A NICE LITTLE NEFARIOUS PLAN WITH WHICH YOU CAN ASSIST ME...

DO TELL US PAPA!

WHISPER WHISPER WHISPER WHISPER

YES

YES

YES

317

WE UNDERSTAND PERFECTLY PAPA ... LEAVE IT TO US

EXTREMELY EXCELLENT MY BOYS

LOBEY IS VISITING CONSTITUENTS A FEW MILES FROM CALTON CREEK...

THAT'S THEM A' VISITED ... WE'LL GET AWA HAME NOO ELFIE!

WHIT ABOOT WUR POST WAR CREDITS?

?

GI BRIDE

318

AT THE OLD FORT IN THE FOOTHILLS...

I HAVE RUN OUT OF BATS FOR MY OFFICE ... I SHALL STOP AT THIS OLD FORT OVERNIGHT AND REPLENISH MY STOCK...

LATER, IN THE RAFTERS...

THERE! MY BAT TRAP IS SET. NOW. I SHALL AWAIT RESULTS...

EMILY HERE'S GOT MEN IN HER BELFRY...

5

MEANTIME...

THERE THE FORT...

THERR THE FORT, THE MAN SAYS...

Bud NEILL

JIST GO RIGHT IN... YE'LL FIN' STRAW IN THE DUNGEON-AN' MIND THE RATS... GUID NIGHT!

GULP...

A NIGHT IN THE FORT WILL DAE THEM NAE HERM...TAKE SOME O' THE CHEEK OOT THEM, BUT...

PERTICK?

INSIDE THE FORT...

I'VE READ ABOOT GUTTERIN' CAUNLES, BUT THAT'S NO' WHIT I'D CRY THIS WAN... RUN DOON TAE THE DUNGEON AN' GET THE STRAW...

AWA' AN' WHIT WIS THAT?

WOOO

NEILL 6

CREAK!

SOUNDS LIKE MITHER'S BAD KNEE ON A WET DAY...

MIND THE CAUN'LE GREASE ON MA GUID BLOUSE, YOU!

OUTSIDE THE OLD FORT A PALE MOON SHINES FITFULLY THRO' THE SCUDDING CLOUDS. SOMEWHERE FAR OFF A LONE COYOTE HOWLS, AND A CHILL WIND RUSTLES THE SCANTY FOLIAGE OF THE STUNTED SHRUBS IN THE GRAVEYARD...

IN OTHER WORDS: IT IS ALTOGETHER ONE HECK OF AN EVENING...

FROM BEHIND A TOMBSTONE...

!

7

Scunns

CREAK!

AW, CUT THE KIDOLOGY ...LISTEN!

WE'LL NO' MIND ABOOT THE STRAW ...NAE YIS O' WUR GOIN' AWA' DOON TAE THE DUNGEON AT THIS TIME O' NIGHT

WE SHOULDA PIT ON WUR AULD CLAES...

YE'R TELLIN' TONY

SOUNDS LIKE A DOOR SQUEAKIN'

MAYBE IT'S THE MAN TAE COLLECT THE MENAGE

WISH YE MEANT IT...

8

THIS IS THE VOICE OF DOOM...

Bud NEILL

EH?

I NEVER SPOKE

DAWN IN CALTON CREEK...

TO THE OLD FORT →

HELP!

?

SOMEBODY CALLIN' FOR HELP...IT CAME FAE UP ON THE ROOF...

BUD NEILL

25

HULP!

TWO AT A TIME

ON THE ROOF OF THE FORT...

VON STOP NEARER UNT—

THERRS ONLY WAN THING FOR IT NOO —KICK HIM IN THE TEETH AN' CHANCE IT...

BUD NEILL

26

BASH!

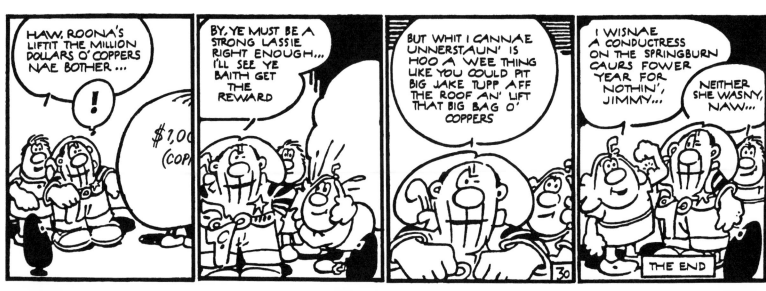

IN THE BLACK HILLS of SOUTH DAKOTA A WANDERING BAND of COMANCHES IS HOLDING A POW-WOW...

UGH
UGH
UGH
UGH
UGH

OBVIOUSLY A GARRULOUS TYPE AMONGST THEM...

HEAP NO RAIN FOR HEAP LONG TIME... HEAP DRY IS HEAP LAND... HEAP BUFFALO ARE HEAP THIRSTY... HEAP THINGS IS HEAP BAD... HEAP HEAP...

HOORAY!

BIG RAIN GOD IS HEAP ANGRY... BIG RAIN GOD HE DRY UP HEAP...

WHICH HEAP DID BIG RAIN GOD HEAP DRY UP?

REMIND ME TO SCALP YOU AFTER THE POW-WOW, EAGLE FEET... TO CONTINUE... BIG RAIN GOD HE HEAP ANGRY... BIG RAIN GOD ASKS FOR SACRIFICE... CALL THE MEDICINE-MAN WHO WILL GIVE US THE HEAP GEN.

HOI, DOC! YOO HOO, DOC!

HEAP WEE HEAP

HEAP BIG HEAP

1

IN THE WELL-KNOWN OFFICE OF THE WELL-KNOWN SHERIFF OF CALTON CREEK, MR LOBEY DOSSER...

SHERIFF

A LETTER FAE THE GLESCA CORPORATION AGREEIN' TAE SELL US AN AULD TRAM FOR A FIVER. 'THE TRAM,' IT SAYS 'A RID WAN, IS ON ITS WAY TO YOU AN' WE HOPE IT PROVES SATISFACTORY IN EVERY RESPECT' IS THAT NO' NICE?

A RID CAUR! A RID GLESCA CAUR FLEEIN' UP AN' DOON THE CALTON CREEK HIGH STREET! IT'LL JIST SEEM LIKE BEIN' AT HAME...

AH, WEEL ... NEED TAE GET THE RAILS LAID AN' THE ELECTRIC FIXED UP READY... ANDY, THE FARRIER, CAN FIX DOON THE RAILS AND WEE SHUG THE PLUMBER CAN MAKE THE STOPS... A RID CAUR... MY, MY...

2

AN EDUCATED OLD JOKER IS RANKIE B., ESQ...

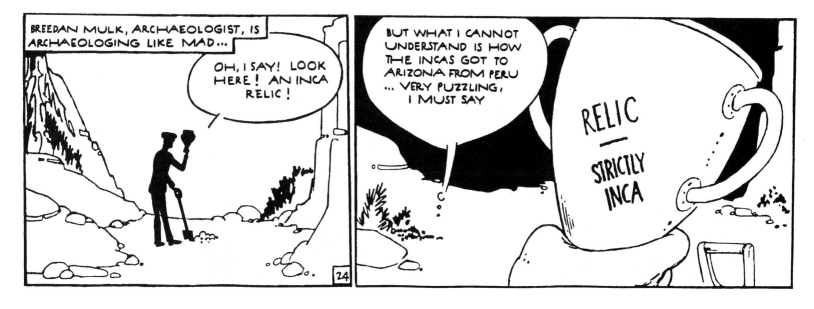

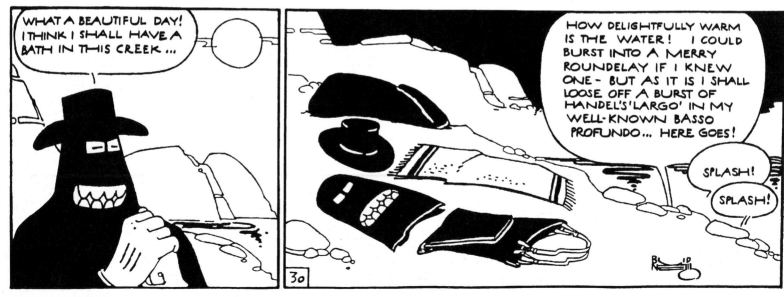

INTO CALTON CREEK GALLOPS A NICE HORSE CONTAINING ONE EXCITED COWBOY...

45

I SAW ELFIE BEIN' LED NORTH BY TWO INJUNS A COUPLA DAYS BACK... SOMETHIN' IN A SACK ON HER SADDLE, TOO...

IT'D BE LOBEY!

WE MUST GO IN PURSUIT...

AT THE TOOT...

WE CAN'T ALL GO AFTER THE INJUNS THERE AIN'T ENOUGH HORSES...

AW, THE SHAME!

TAKE THE CAUR

DON'T BE DAFT! THERE IS NAEBODY CAN PULL IT...

ONE MOMENT, PLEASE! MY HAT IS AN ATOMIC CHAPEAU... WITH IT I CAN GENERATE ALL SORTS OF ELECTRICITY... THE PROBLEM OF THE CAR IS SOLVED... LET US GO IN PURSUIT!

GOOD OLD STARK!

ATTA BOY!

BRAVO!

46

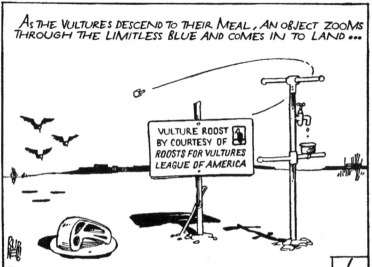

19

20

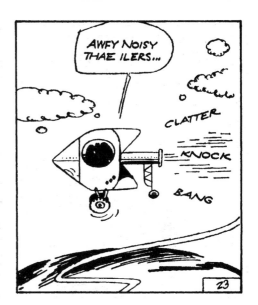

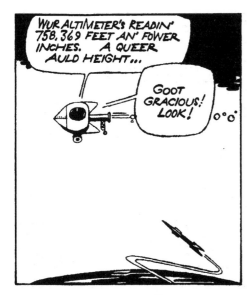

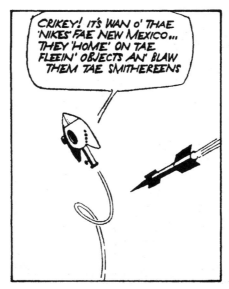

MIRACULOUSLY THROWN CLEAR OF THE EXPLODING SHIP, LOBEY IS HURLED THROUGH SPACE UNTIL ...

WELL, THAT DIDNAE HAUF AERATE MA WHISKERS! NOO, WHAUR'S THIS?

SPOOKY KINNA PLACE ... HULLO! ONYBODY HAME?

NAW!

27

THE ECHOES IS GOOD AROON' HERE ... I'LL TRY SHOUTIN' AGAIN ... HULLO! COME OOT YE'RE SPIED...

YE'LL GO TAE THE BAD FIRE...

FOR TELLIN' FIBS...

BURNY BURNY...

? ? ?

HOW'S YIR MITHER'S SAIR LEG?

AWA' HAME... YIR TEA'S OOT!

28

35

36

37

38

41

42

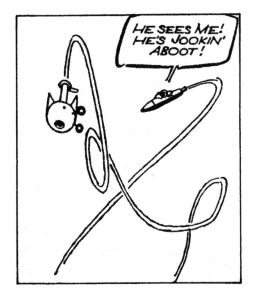

57

58

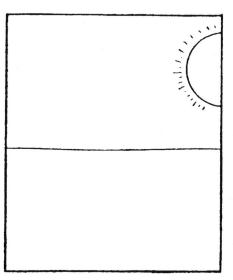

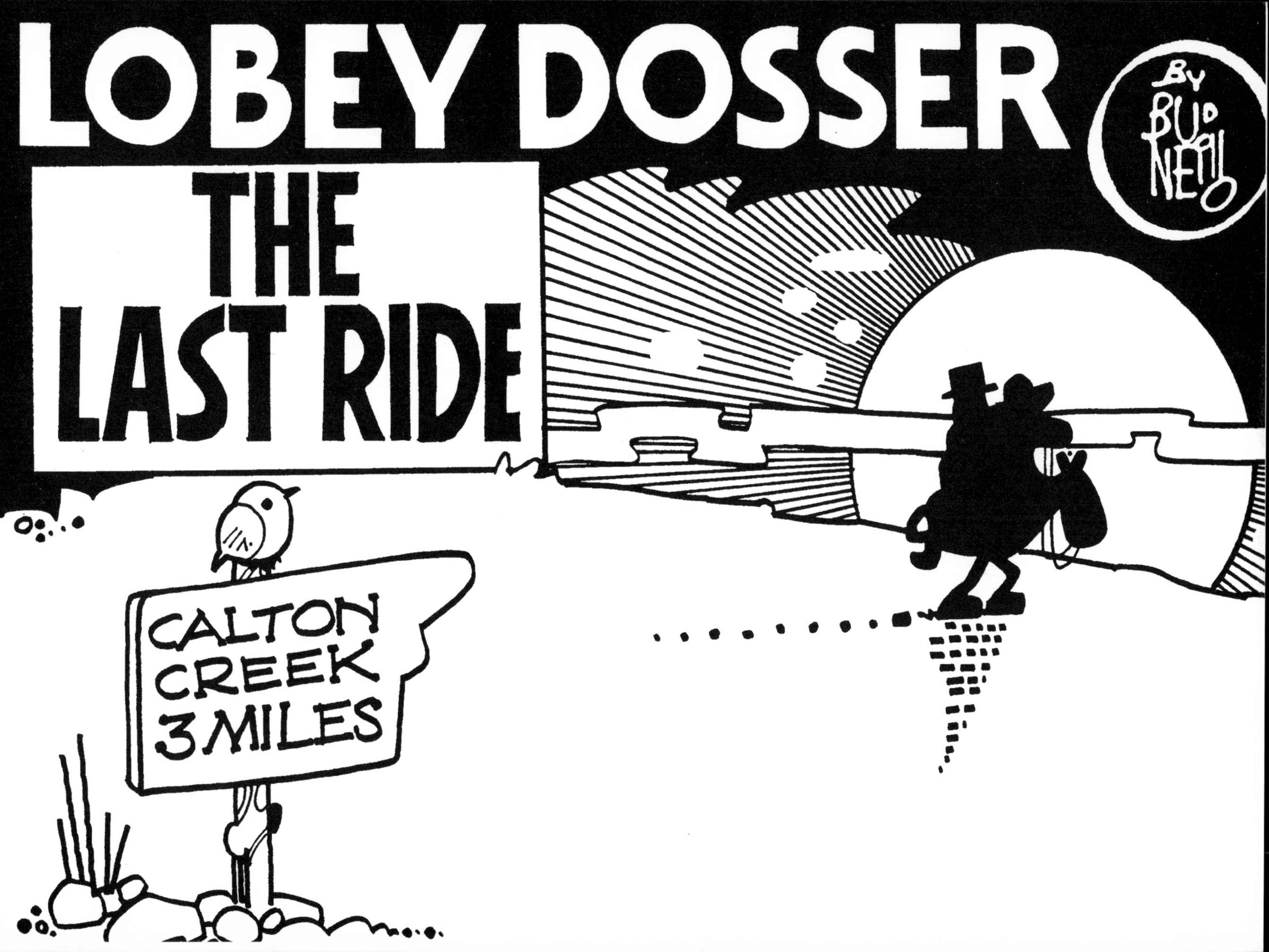
LOBEY DOSSER
BY BUD NEILL
THE LAST RIDE
CALTON CREEK 3 MILES

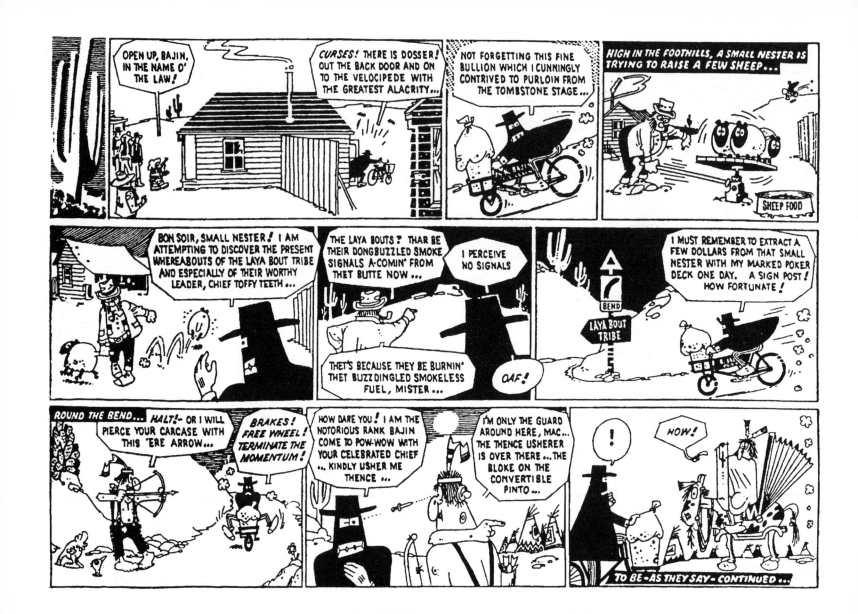

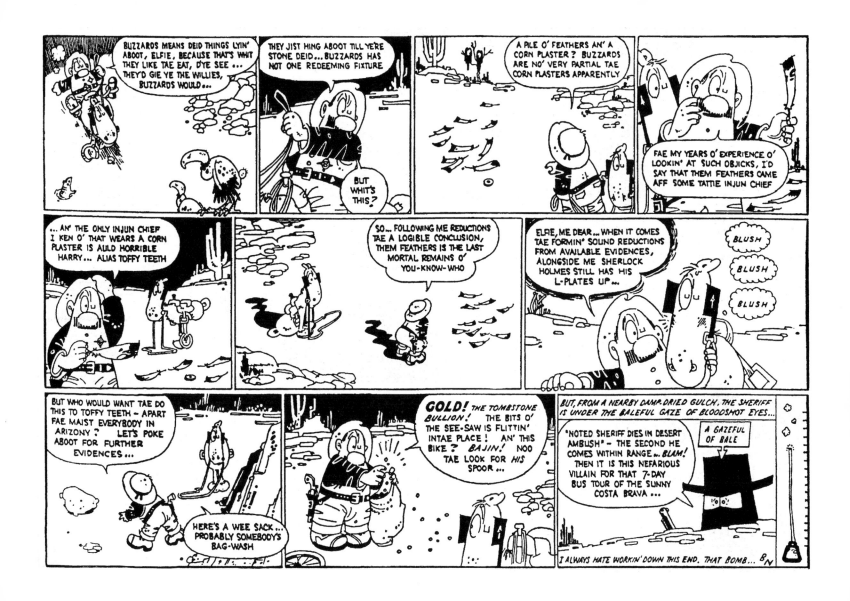

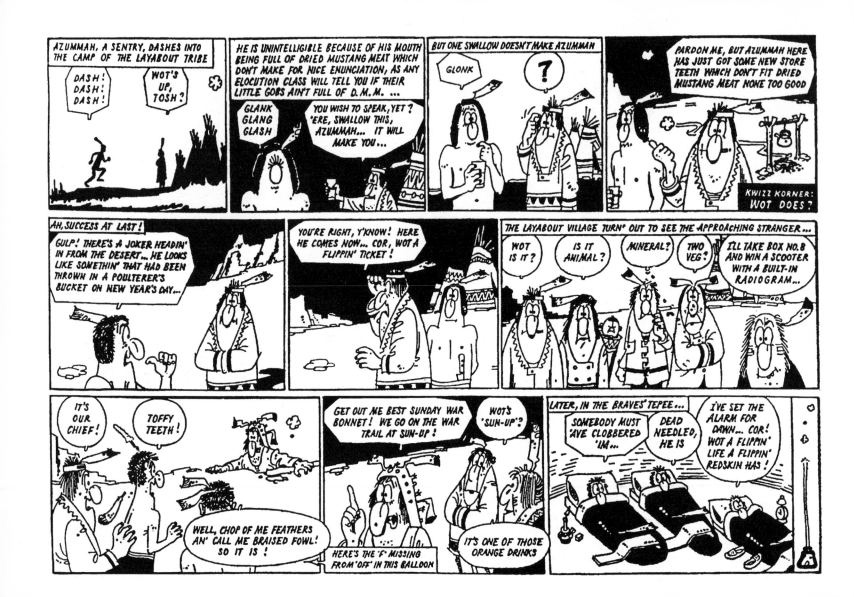

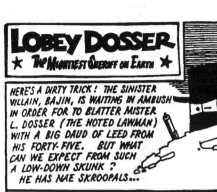

LOBEY DOSSER
★ The Mightiest Sheriff on Earth ★

HERE'S A DIRTY TRICK! THE SINISTER VILLAIN, BAJIN, IS WAITING IN AMBUSH IN ORDER FOR TO BLATTER MISTER L. DOSSER (THE NOTED LAWMAN) WITH A BIG DAUD OF LEED FROM HIS FORTY-FIVE. BUT WHAT CAN WE EXPECT FROM SUCH A LOW-DOWN SKUNK? HE HAS NAE SKROOPALS...

C'MON, ELFIE, LET'S HIT THE TRAIL BACK TAE THE CREEK WITH THIS SACK O' BULLION...

ALTHOUGH I CANNAE FIGGER HOO BAJIN COULD GO AN' LEAVE A MILLION IN GOLD LYIN' ABOOT A SILLY AULD DESERT. MAYBE HE...

BEE-OINC!

A RISHYCOOTED BULLET! DOON FOR YIR LIFE, HEN, AN' DON'T MOVE...

WHUMPH!

ZEE-DONK!

WHEE-UHM!

CANNAE SEE A BLOOMIN' THING ... I'LL TRY THE OLD HAT CAPER ... HERE'S A WEE STICK...

NAE DICE! MAYBE THE RASCAL'S SCARPERED...

?

I'LL TAKE A SQUINT...

KAR-OW

A MAIST HAZARDY OCCUPATION IS THIS SHERIFF LARK...

HE'S RIGHT, Y'KNOW...

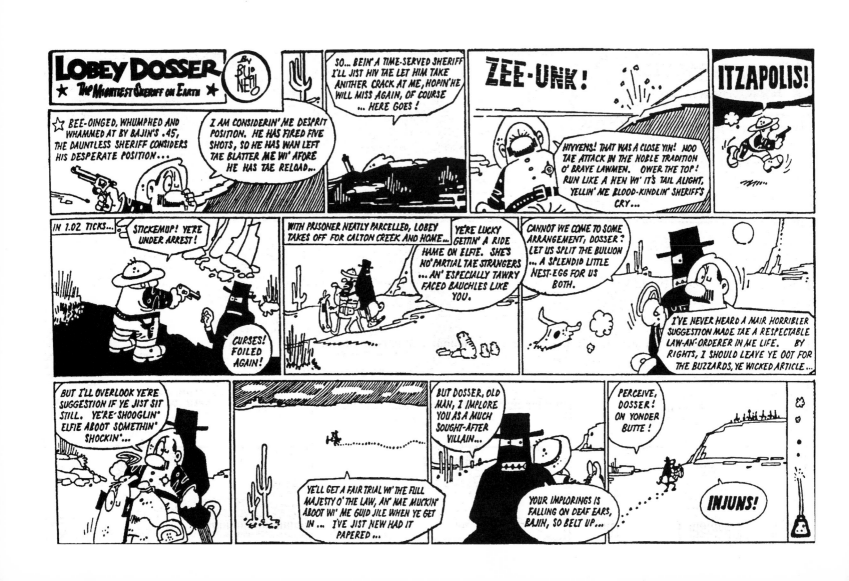

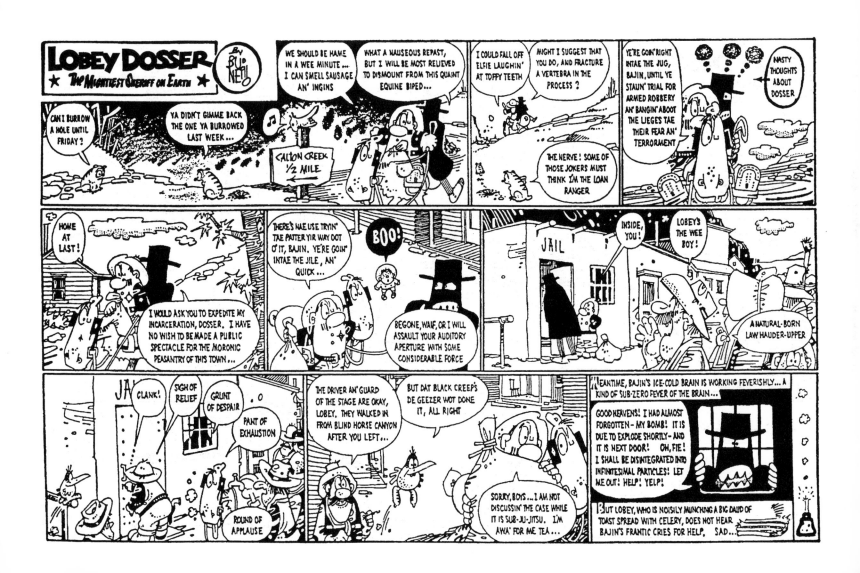

LOBEY DOSSER
★ The Mightiest Sheriff on Earth ★
By Bud Neill

LEAVING THE DOOMED RANK BAJIN TO BE CRUSHED BY THE TERRIBLE DEADFALL, LET US TODAY TAKE A BUTCHERS AT SOME OTHER WELL-KNOWN GEEZERS +++ LOBEY, F'RINSTANCE

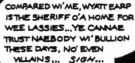

COMPARED WI' ME, WYATT EARP IS THE SHERIFF O' A HOME FOR WEE LASSIES... YE CANNAE TRUST NAEBODY WI' BULLION THESE DAYS, NO' EVEN VILLANS... *SIGH...*

A GLESS O' PORT NOO AN' AGAIN IS VERY GOOD FOR FIGHTIN' CRIMINAL ELEMENTS WI'... IT STEADIES THE NERVES AN' HELPS TAE KEEP THE RED CORPSICLES CORPSICLIN' ROON' THE BODY... SOMEBODY COMIN' – HIDE THE BOTTLE IN CASE IT'S WEANS... COME IN!

FIE, MISTER DOSSER, TUT, TUT, TUT I'M NO' EXACTLY AFF ME NUT... TO SUCH DECEIT *YOU* SHOULD RESORT! I SAW YOU HIDE AWAY THE PORT... COME NOW, YOUR CUPBOARD PLEASE UNLATCH AN' LET US POUR WAN DOON THE HATCH

GLUG, GLUG, GREAT STUFF, A REAL WEE TREAT! (A GILL WID CA' YE AFF YIR FEET...) AND NOW THE NEWS AT SIX O'CLOCK... ME BOYS IS HOME – THEY'RE OUT OF HOCK! IT SEEMS BY BAJIN THEY WERE FOUND, HE SENT THEM HOME ALL SAFE AND SOUND... BUT YET THEY SAY THEIR LIVES HE SAVED WHEN COCK-EYED REDSKIN, MIND DEPRAVED, PULLED PROP FROM 'NEATH A GREAT BIG LOG WHICH BASHED OLD RANKIE ON THE NOG... 'RUN, BOYS, RUN!' THEY SAY HE SHOUTED, BEFORE HE WAS SO FOULLY CLOUTED...

WEB-FOOTED PETE
DEAD OR ALIVE

INTERVAL
4 OUR
NATURE QUIZ

THIS IS A WHAT?

↑ANSWER IN END PANEL

IT'S NO' LIKE BAJIN TAE GET HEROICAL... MAYBE THE SUN'S TOUCHED HIS HEID... I'LL INVESTIGATE THE MATTER THE NOO...

THE BOYS ARE FINE... A WEE BIT THINNER... I'D BETTER GO AN' GET THEIR DINNER

ON THE TRAIL TO THE DEADFALL...

THE WEANS IS GIVIN' YE TOO MANY SWEETIES, ELFIE... GETTIN' FAT'S A PUGGY...

WELL, HERE'S THE DEADFALL RIGHT ENOUGH, BUT NAE SIGNS O' LIFE – NO' TAE MENTION ME BULLION

MOAN

DRAP YIR GUN AN' COME OOT WI' YIR HAUNS UP!

OF COURSE! AN ARIZONA SPEUG FEEDING IT'S YOUNG...

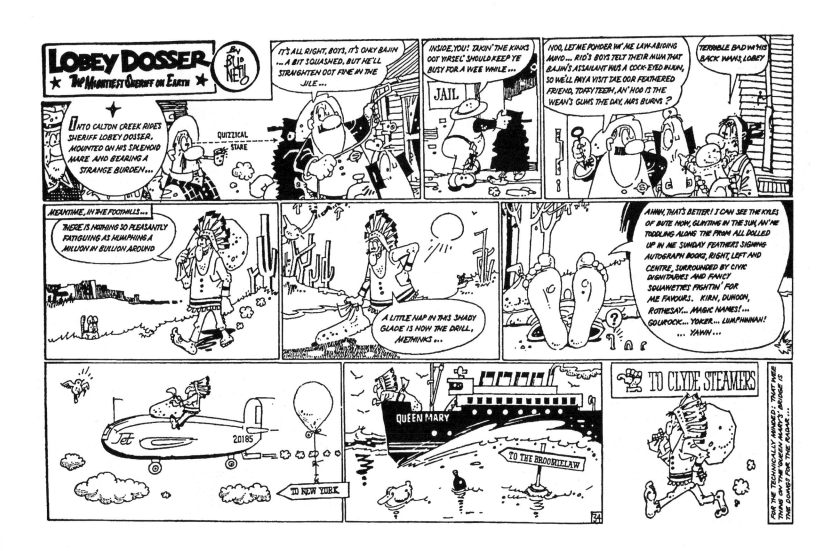

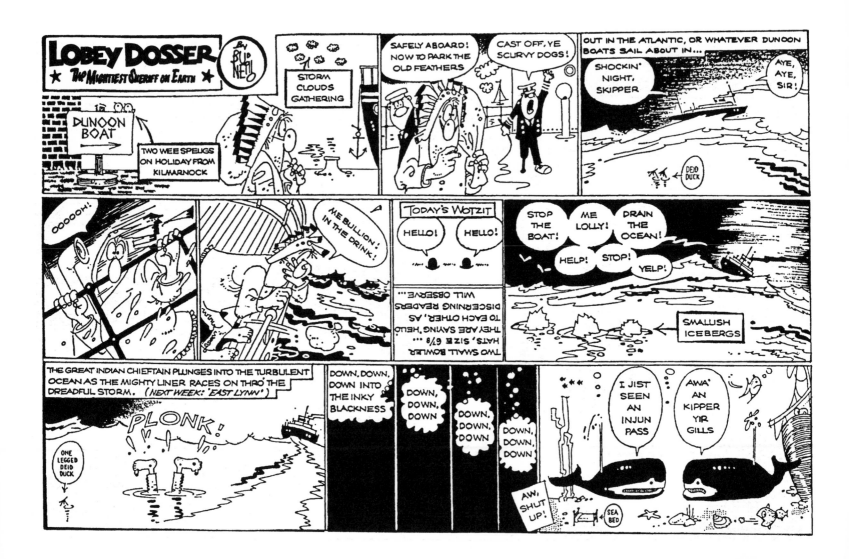

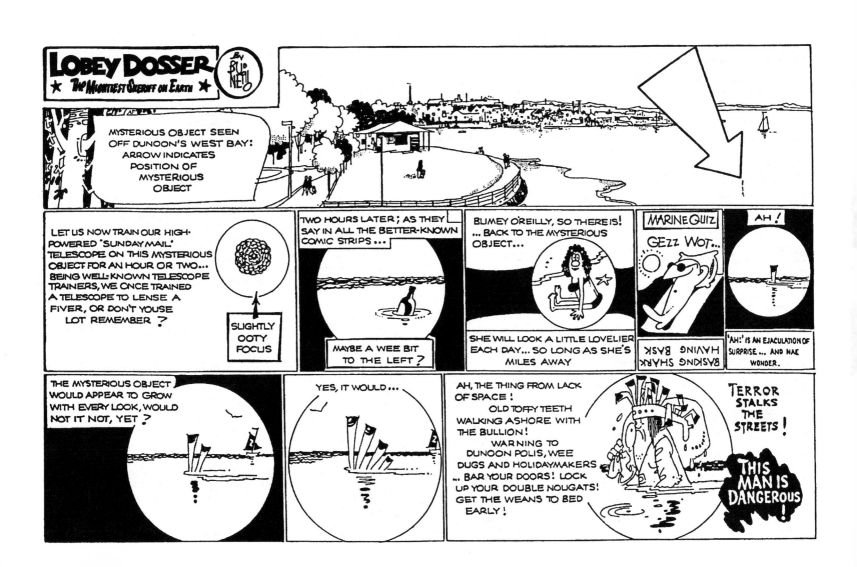

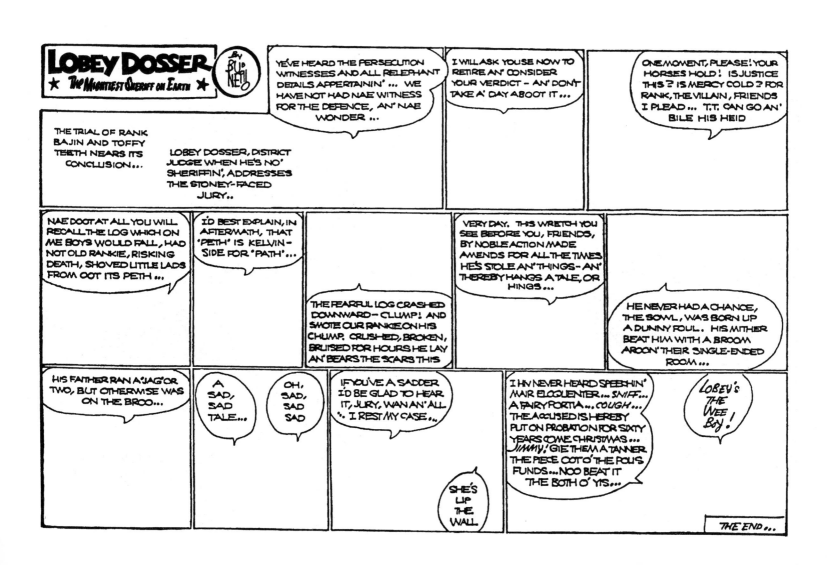